JESUS LOVES ME
All the time

Ninth Printing, 1990

written by E. Elaine Watson

illustrated by Lorraine Arthur

Library of Congress Catalog Card No. 83-051633

©1984. The STANDARD PUBLISHING Company, Cincinnati, Ohio
Division of STANDEX INTERNATIONAL Corporation. Printed in U.S.A.

Jesus loves me, this is true,
Wherever I am or whatever I do.

Jesus loves me at lunchtime,
playtime,
bedtime,
anytime,
everytime,
all the time.
That's when Jesus loves me.

When I am climbing up a tree,

Or when I am swimming in the sea,
Jesus loves me.

When I am walking down the street,

Or when I am sitting in my seat,
Jesus loves me.

When I cry for my broken toy,

Or when I am laughing and full of joy,
Jesus loves me.

He loves me at lunchtime,
breakfasttime,
suppertime,
anytime,
everytime,
all the time.
That's when Jesus loves me.

When I am riding around on my bike,

Or when Daddy helps me fly my kite,
Jesus loves me.

When I am feeding bread to my duck,

Or when I share my brand-new truck,
Jesus loves me.

Jesus loves me at lunchtime,
summertime,
wintertime,
anytime,
everytime,
all the time.
That's when Jesus loves me.

Jesus loves me, this is true,
Wherever I am, or whatever I do.
And I want to love Jesus all the time, too.

I'll love Him at lunchtime,
breakfasttime,
suppertime,
playtime,
wintertime,
summertime,
bedtime,
anytime,
everytime,
all the time.

That's when I want to love Jesus,
Because that's when Jesus loves me.